Discovering Identity Through Intimacy

Who You Are, Why You're Here and Where You're Going

Edited By: Helen Crews

Cover Art by: Jalynn Webb

ISBN: 979-8-9938071-2-6

May your understanding of intimacy be transformed and your identity be renewed.

Table of Contents

Introduction

Who I am, Why I'm Here and Where I'm going are found in Jesus. My eyes opened to the truth of that statement around 2022. A couple of years leading up to that time, I found myself consistently going to God in prayer about purpose. Some of the questions I asked were:

God, what am I here for? Why did you put me on this earth? What's my purpose?! I would get so frustrated because I didn't hear or sense an answer, and of course, we can't rush God, so I had to **wait**. Wait until He chose to make it clear. Wait for some sense of direction. Then one day, while in devotion, something clicked. The thought *God is probably going to have me at a relationship conference, telling people all the wrong things to do in marriage. I'll be that person…* crossed my mind. I laughed briefly to myself, and then it was like God responded by saying, *"No, that's not it. The issue is not divorce or marriage, it's identity. If you would have known who you were at that time, the marriage wouldn't have happened in the first place."*

That thought sobered me. I wasn't laughing anymore. The Lord handed me a new lens to look back at past decisions, relationships, and beliefs about myself. I latched onto that identity thought. I interrogated it, and it set fire in my spirit. Ignorance of who God is and who He says we are leads to decisions that create unnecessary turmoil in life. Culture coined the phrase *ignorance is bliss*. That couldn't be further from the truth. The Word says *My people are destroyed for lack of knowledge [of My law, where I reveal My will]…* (**Hosea 4:6 AMP**). The areas in which we are ignorant, we will suffer. While navigating the aftermath of divorce, I decided to get acquainted with God on a more personal level. I was pleasantly surprised to find that the more I learned about Him, the more I discovered myself. Slowly, He began to reveal to me that life's deepest questions are realized in Him. Before moving on to Part I, I dare you to declare *out loud*: *Who I am, Why I'm Here and Where I'm Going are found in Jesus*! Say it one more time for the people in the back! Now, let's get to work!

Part I: Who I Am, Why I'm Here & Where I'm Going...

What's the first thing that comes to mind when you read the word **identity**? When you heard that word in the past, what was the context? If I were to ask you what you believe about your own identity, how would you answer that question? Would you have a hard time responding? This may seem like an abrupt start, but identity is the thread that keeps our decisions, desires, and these very pages together.

There's meaning behind the title of this section, so let's break it down:

Who I am (**identity**) – how you see and define yourself.

Why I'm here (**assignment**) – what God desires for you to be focused on in this season.

Where I'm going (**path**) – the Lord's path for you to fulfill the calling and assignments in your life.

Key Scripture: **Gen. 1:27 (AMP)** *So God created man in His own image, in the image and likeness of God He created him; male and female He created them.*

The dictionary defines likeness as the fact or quality of being alike; resemblance. One of the synonyms is identity.

That same passage can be read as, *So God created man in His own image, in the image and [identity] of God He created him; male and female He created them.*

There are a lot of definitions of identity, but Merriam-Webster sums it up the best: "the distinguishing character or personality of an individual and the condition of being the same with something described or asserted." The Bible makes it clear that we are made in the image and identity of God. He created humankind to reflect His nature, qualities, and will on the earth. A feat that cannot be done without knowing Him. *So, who is He?* Consider the essence of God's character below:

He is love and He loves: **1 John 4: 7-12 (NIV)**

He's holy: **1 Peter 1:15 (NIV)**

He's mindful: **Psalm 8:4 (NIV)**

He's faithful: **1 Thessalonians 5:24 (NIV)**

He's consistent: **Hebrews 13:8 (NIV)**

He's forgiving: **Colossians 3:13 (NIV)**

He's compassionate: **Psalm 103:13 (AMP)**

He's patient: **2 Peter 3: 9 (NIV)**

He's kind: **Romans 11:22 (NIV)**

He's present: **Exodus 33:14 (NIV)**

This is not an exhaustive list – *God is* so much more than this. Read the Scriptures associated with each characteristic and be prepared to discuss your thoughts. Feel free to use the space below for any comments or questions you'd like to share.

Part II: Cultivating a Relationship with God

Part I provided clarity on identity and the character of God, but now let's go deeper. Getting closer to Jesus and learning to trust Him happens through a relationship. Think about it practically – you know, love and trust your friends because you've spent time with them. You've learned their mannerisms, what makes them happy, and when they're bothered because of the investment you've made in the relationship. You can hear the advice they'd give you, even when they're not present, because you've grown together. You trust them with secrets and choose to work through difficulties because they're safe for the healed and wounded parts of you. The root that produces flourishing friendships is choosing to cultivate a relationship. Jesus desires the same.

God longs for a relationship with you because He is a relational God. **Joshua 1:9** says, *This is my command—be strong and courageous! Do not be afraid or discouraged. For the LORD your God is with you wherever you go*. God said this to Joshua at a time of transition – Moses was deceased and it was time for Joshua to lead the second generation of Israelites into the Promised Land. He is both encouraging and reassuring Joshua that He is the God that does not leave, but goes with you *wherever* you go.

King David speaks of his relationship with God throughout the Old Testament, and **Psalm 32:5** is a good verse to examine. *Then I acknowledged my sin to You and did not cover up my iniquity. I said, I will confess my transgressions to the LORD, and You forgave the guilt of my sin*. In verse 7, he continues," *You are my hiding place; You will protect me from trouble and surround me with songs of deliverance*." Read Psalm 32 in its entirety and be prepared to discuss it with the group.

This psalm is a snapshot of a relationship with a holy and forgiving God. It is also a picture of *repentance*. Repentance is a word that is often misconstrued, depending on your exposure and understanding of God and the church. Repentance is not remorse. Remorse tends to be grounded in emotion, but the tricky thing is that it looks like repentance: the tears, sadness, and a feeble attempt to right the wrong. Yet, no matter how sorry the offender is in that moment, remorse falls short of a changed heart. *Why is a changed heart important*? Because without it, the offense will likely be repeated. A person may *feel* sorry, but that is not synonymous with change.

In contrast, repentance is a changed heart and mind. There may be some emotion when a person repents, but the emotion is not the foundation. Instead, the foundation is a desire to please God, which leads to a **new choice.** A choice to turn away from the sin that needed to be repented for. For example, when I was younger, I was sexually active with my then-boyfriend. Once I got baptized and came into the knowledge of Christ, whenever I engaged in sexual activity, I would feel conviction or God making me aware of my sin, and even remorse. On several occasions I cried after engaging in sexual acts with that individual because I knew our actions grieved God. My heart was heavy. I knew I needed to stop. Yet, a heavy heart didn't mean a changed heart. If you find yourself in a similar situation, whether it's sex or something else, *know that God is gracious*. He wants you to come to Him, even in the midst of dysfunctional cycles and unwise choices.

This is best seen in *Samuel's Farewell Speech*, found in the first book of Samuel. The Prophet addresses Israel corporately for the final time because they no longer want him to lead them. Their demand is for a king (see **1 Samuel 8:19-20**). God appoints a king even though it goes against His plan, and Samuel makes that clear in chapter 12.

You have done all this evil; yet do not turn away from the LORD, *but serve the* LORD *with all your heart.* ²¹ *Do not turn away after useless idols. They can do you no good, nor can they rescue you, because they are useless.* ²² *For the sake of His great name the* LORD *will not reject His people, because the* LORD *was pleased to make you His own* (**1 Samuel 12:20-22 NIV**).

No matter what you chose to do yesterday or what you're planning to do today, you are still made in the image of God. It pleased Him to create you and to breathe His life into you. Just as Samuel's words echoed in the ears of the Israelites then, I pray they echo in your ears now: repent, turn to God, and serve Him alone.

When it comes to the importance of cultivating a relationship with Christ, it's impossible to do so without repentance. Repentance is so integral to the Christian faith that you won't receive the Holy Spirit without it (see **Acts 2:37-38**). Repentance opens your eyes to sin and your need for Jesus. Psalms, Joshua, and many other books in the Bible demonstrate an intimate relationship between God and man. God is not a faraway entity sitting behind the clouds, but He is a parent, friend, husband, comforter, helper, and so much more. He is an ever-present God and as you come close to Him, He responds by drawing nearer to you (**James 4:8**). So many people in the Bible were able to enjoy a relationship with God because they spent time with Him continually. They chose to prioritize intimacy with Him, and you will witness the fruit of that decision when you read the Word for yourself.

Notes from the author:

Before going further, I want to give context to the word intimacy. For most of my life, I defined intimacy as a sexual encounter with my significant other or spouse. While sex is an *expression* of intimacy, that is no longer how I define it. My understanding of the word is borrowed from Pastor Jerry Flowers, Jr. - intimacy means *into me I see.* It's deciding to engage in emotional nakedness, which means choosing to show up authentically in a relationship: not just with your strengths, but weaknesses, scars, and fears. It's choosing to bring transparency and vulnerability with you instead of leaving them locked in the vaults of your heart. I realize that this is no small task and can feel terrifying, but it's worth it. What grieves me most is that many have never experienced true intimacy because their definition is wrapped in bedroom sheets. As was the case for me throughout my four and a half years of marriage. It took for that relationship to die for me to get to the point where I was ready to invite Jesus into the deep recesses of my heart. Only then did my perspective of intimacy evolve. Jesus responds to my fears by ministering to my heart and showing me that He'll never leave nor give up on me. He responds to my vulnerability through His gentle kindness and presence. He responds to my brokenness by covering me and revealing through His Word that I am worthy of love. Jesus set the bar for intimacy in my life; Pastor Flowers, Jr. simply provided language for it. My prayer is that you will experience true intimacy, not just in your relationships with friends or your spouse, but first in your covenant with Jesus.

In order to gain a new perspective on developing intimacy with God, first consider why it's important. Growing deeper in a relationship with anyone requires time, consistency, and sacrifice. *So, is it worth it?* While it's encouraging to read or hear about other people's relationship with Jesus, what does your relationship look like?

*Activity: Read the following questions and answer in the space provided:

1. What word(s) describe your current relationship with God?

_____

_____

_____

_____

2. I cultivate intimacy with Jesus by,

_____

_____

_____

_____

_____

3. How does your love, affection, and respect for Jesus compare with that of your friends, loved ones, or significant other?

_____

_____

_____

_____

4. T/F I desire to have a deep relationship with Jesus just as I have deep relationships with others in my life.

Part III: Identity and Impact

What's the point of putting yourself through the sacrifice and time it takes to invest in a relationship with Jesus? Consider the points below:

1. Discovering God's nature and His plan for your life

2. Understanding the impact of identity in your life

3. Becoming aware of Satan's attacks on identity throughout your life

Point one has to do with the nature of God. He is intentional, mindful, and purposeful in all that He does. We see evidence of this all around us – the way the seasons change and how creation innately knows how and when to respond to the shifting of time. His intentionality is also witnessed in your anatomy. At this moment, your heart is pumping blood, carrying oxygen to your cells, and providing essential nutrients to your organs. There are systems at work within you that aid in alertness, regulation of body temperature, digestion, and much more. None of this is by coincidence or happenstance. It is the result of the omniscient God who knew what your body would need to function and support you before you took your first breath.

He didn't stop at nature and anatomy, but your personality, gifts, family, region of birth, birth date, and all the things that shape you were divinely chosen by God. The influence you have and the things that come naturally to you were established as He knit you together in your mother's womb. Even the things that agitate you were handpicked by the Lord. You may have read that last sentence and thought to yourself, *'Huh? Even the things that agitate me?'* The short answer to that question is, "Yes!" Pastor, Author, and Coach Dr. Dharius Daniels speaks to this in his book *Your Purpose is Calling – Your Difference is Your Destiny.*

> "What irritates you? … I'm talking about those situations and circumstances that truly bother you…What makes your blood boil? Pay attention to whatever comes to mind, because they could be important. Here's a principle: the problems that agitate you the most are more than likely the problems you were created to solve" (Daniels, 2022).

Notice the distinction he's making. He's not talking about life's ordinary irritants that come from co-workers, family, and friends. He's referring to the things that frustrate you to the point of passion and action to change it. There is likely an assignment in that irritation that God placed there *just for you.*

*Activity: Without using a dictionary, how would you define purpose, assignment, and calling? Answer in the space provided below:

Purpose:

_____

_____

_____

_____

_____

_____

Assignment:

_____

_____

_____

_____

_____

_____

_____

Calling:

_____

_____

_____

_____

_____

_____

_____

How do purpose, calling, and assignment differ?

_____

_____

_____

_____

_____

_____

_____

The pursuit of purpose can be a challenging one because, as stated in the introduction, I had a season of seeking God about my purpose. I prayed about it repeatedly and was often left frustrated. On top of that, when I read the accounts of faith-filled individuals in the Bible, none of them had seasons of asking God what their purpose was. They all seemed to be living their lives and the Lord came to them with His presence, instruction, and encouragement when it was time for them to act. Did they know something I didn't? Was I conflating purpose with something else? I chose to listen to teachings on the topic of purpose, and they led me right back to the Word. Here's what I discovered:

Purpose: If you have received Jesus as your Lord and Savior, then you are under the unified purpose of the church, which is broken up into two parts. The first is to *go and make disciples of all nations, baptizing them in the name of the Father and of the Son and of the Holy Spirit, and teaching them to obey everything I have commanded you…* (**Matthew 28:19 and 20 NIV**). This text is known as the Great Commission, and Jesus is speaking to His disciples after His crucifixion, resurrection and appearance to them. Not long after this, He ascends to heaven to take His place at the right hand of the Father.

God mandates us to make disciples of believers, helping them mature in their trust and obedience to God. The second component of purpose is to spread the good news of the gospel to those who are still lost and living without the hope of Jesus. In Mark 16, Jesus is speaking to His disciples and He states in verses 15 and 16, *Go into all the world and preach the gospel to all creation. Whoever believes and is baptized will be saved, but whoever does not believe will be condemned.* This is the purpose that all believers have been given by God to steward. If purpose is the destination, then assignment is the vehicle.

Assignment: Assignment is how purpose is fulfilled and it's unique to the individual. People have many different assignments throughout their lives, and those assignments may change with life transitions or external circumstances. For example, I currently serve as a small group leader for several young women at my local church. This is an assignment that the Lord gave me back in 2020. My co-lead, Sarah and I said yes, and we have been going strong for the last four years. But there will likely be a time when the Lord calls one or both of us to shift. When that happens, the assignment will be complete. Some are assigned to serve as mentors, administrators, missionaries, authors, homemakers, entrepreneurs, producers, workshop facilitators, and the list goes on. The assignment that the Lord wants you to focus on right now will be unique to you: your gifts, your season of life, and your level of obedience. However, it will always achieve God's purpose.

Calling: What does it mean to be called by God? The Apostle Paul talks about calling several times throughout the New Testament. Some of those accounts are listed below:

- Paul in his letter to the church in Ephesus - Therefore I, a prisoner for serving the Lord, beg you to lead a life worthy of your calling, for you have been called by God. **2** Always be humble and gentle. Be patient with each other, making allowance for each other's faults because of your love - **Ephesians 4:1 (NLT)**.

- Paul's second letter to the church in Thessalonica - **11** With this in view, we constantly pray for you, that our God will count you worthy of your **calling** [to faith] and with [His] power fulfill every desire for goodness, and complete [your] every work of faith, **12** so that the name of our Lord Jesus will be glorified in you [by what you do], and you in Him, according to the [precious] grace of our God and the Lord Jesus Christ - **2 Thessalonians 1:11-12 (AMP)**.

- Paul's second letter to his mentee Timothy - …**9** for He delivered us *and* saved us and **called** us with a holy calling [a calling that leads to a consecrated life—a life set apart—a life of purpose], not because of our works [or because of any personal merit—we could do nothing to earn this], but because of His own purpose and grace [His amazing, undeserved favor] which was granted to us in Christ Jesus before the world began [eternal ages ago] - **2 Timothy 1:9 (AMP)**.

- Peter's first letter to the elect living as exiles - **8** Finally, all of you be like-minded [united in spirit], sympathetic, brotherly, kindhearted [courteous and compassionate toward each other as members of one household], and humble in spirit; **9** and never return evil for evil or insult for insult [avoid scolding, berating, and any kind of abuse], but on the contrary, give a blessing [pray for one another's well-being, contentment, and protection]; **for you have been called** for this very purpose, that you might inherit a blessing [from God that brings well-being, happiness, and protection] – **1 Peter 3:8-9 (AMP)**.

Be prepared to discuss your thoughts on the Scriptures listed above. Feel free to use the space below for any comments or questions you'd like to share.

_____

_____

_____

_____

_____

_____

_____

_____

_____

_____

It's clear from Paul's writings that calling comes from the Lord. He makes the decision to call and appoint you to the assignments that He's predestined. God's call on your life is a result of His pursuit of you, not the other way around. **Luke 9** begins with *"Now Jesus **called** together the twelve [disciples] and gave them [the right to exercise] power and authority over all the demons and to heal diseases"* **(AMP)**. The disciples didn't walk up to Jesus and say we want to follow you. Instead, they were pursued and chosen by Jesus: called out of the life they knew for a new life of following Him.

Jesus Himself makes this clear in **John 15** while speaking to His disciples. *You have not chosen Me, but I have chosen you and I have appointed and placed and purposefully planted you, so that you would go and bear fruit and keep on bearing, and that your fruit will remain and be lasting, so that whatever you ask of the Father in My name [as My representative] He may give to you* **(AMP)**. When Jesus calls it's your responsibility to answer. When you say yes to His call your priorities should shift from pursuing your own desires and will for your life, to exalting and fulfilling God's will. Answering His call comes with the process of sanctification or being set apart and holy for God's use, because a life of rebellion makes it hard to hear and surrender to His voice.

The interesting part about calling though, is that it's not just an individual experience, but a collective one as well. *Does Jesus call us all individually like he did the twelve disciples?* Yes. However, those of us who confess Jesus as our Lord and Savior are called to live a life worthy of that call (see **Ephesians 4**). Doing that requires consistent obedience and surrender to God and His Word. Extending compassion, being unified in God's spirit and choosing to be a blessing (see **1 Peter 3**). It requires being in community with people who love Jesus and have answered His call or are seeking to discover His call for their life. It requires the practice of spiritual disciplines, like prayer, worship, giving and fasting. *Will you fall short?* Absolutely. However, Paul teaches that God doesn't take His calling away or change His mind about you. He says in **Romans 11:29 (AMP)**, *For the gifts and the calling of God are irrevocable [for He does not withdraw what He has given, nor does He change His mind about those to whom He gives His grace or to whom He sends His call.* God did not make a mistake when He chose and called you, because He is all-knowing. He knows the plans that He has for you, and He handpicked you (see **Jeremiah 29:11**). When you fall short (because we all do), repent and turn back to Him.

Making your unique difference in the earth is preceded by understanding God's plan for your life. Dr. Daniels coined the phrase, *I don't just want to make a difference, I want to make my difference.* You were not only created to go to work, pay bills, travel, and make social media posts. While there's nothing wrong with those things, God put you on this earth, when and where He did, with your influence and personality *on purpose*. He wants you to know Him as your faithful and present Father and He wants you to discover your gifts and your why. These are only realized through the pursuit of intimacy with Him.

Grasping the significance of identity in your life requires self-examination. The way you see, think and how you speak to yourself directly impacts your behavior. Here's another way to put it – *if you don't have an accurate understanding of God and your identity in Him, it will influence all areas of your life.* One major area is career. Some are currently pursuing jobs, careers, and lifestyles that have nothing to do with the gifts, call, and assignment that God has given them. Yet, their pursuit persists. Maybe due to the influence of social media and a desire for a "soft life." Maybe because of pressure from parents or other family members. Maybe they believe the lie that a career or a certain lifestyle will fulfill them, or at the very least, give them access to all the things that will. The hard truth is that oftentimes, their constant pursuit pulls them away from God and true fulfillment. Possessions, recognition, and status are temporary at best and will never be enough. I've heard stories of those who forsook all else to drink from the well of their dreams, only to be left with an unquenched thirst and relentless loneliness.

Use the space below for any comments and/or questions you have on the relationship between career and identity.

_____

_____

_____

_____

_____

_____

_____

_____

_____

A misguided sense of identity also impacts relationships. Some individuals remain loyal to friends for decades – reverencing the 'no new friends' and 'ride or die' rhetoric of culture. When one of the ways the Lord matures, encourages, and delivers clarity to His people is through relationships. Without this realization, it's easy to resist the very people the Lord wants to use to draw them closer to Himself.

If this is evident in platonic relationships, then know that the same is true in romantic contexts. Many get into relationships and settle because they don't know their value and worth. They never took time to assess their needs and values or establish relational standards and non-negotiables. Their eyes are blind to how precious and loved they are, unaware of what they carry on the inside. So inevitably, they enter a relationship with someone who's also unaware of their value, worth, and needs. The blind lead the blind down a path of unnecessary suffering and heartache.

This is a road that I know far too well. I mentioned in Part I that I was previously married. I met that young man when I was 15 years old on Myspace – *who remembers that?* After about seven or eight years of on-and-off dating, we decided to get married. When I look back at those years, the immaturity, selfishness, insecurity, lustfulness, and blatant unawareness are evident. Most of my value and worth were wrapped up in that relationship: the compliments we got from outsiders, the feelings he kindled, the words he spoke or didn't speak, his affection or lack thereof, his disposition and reactions towards me.

What I've come to realize is that my identity was misplaced. If I would've spent half of that time cultivating my relationship with God:

- Reading His Word and asking Him to show me myself.

- Seeking community with people who embrace their God-given identity and could speak life into mine.

- Being curious about how God defines marriage and what He desires for and from it.

If I would have examined how God loves, honors, and leads His bride, the church, and allowed His Word to take precedence over my ex's words, then that chapter of my life would have looked much different. By rearranging my priorities, *God Himself* would have led me in creating relational standards and non-negotiables. His Word would have shaped my values and self-worth. I would have discovered the kind of relational treatment that pleases Him and the kind that goes directly against His heart. Knowing what I know now, I would have never entered into a covenant with or even dated that individual for as long as I did. If you're curious about God's stance on relationships, consider the Scriptures below:

Psalm 1:1 (AMP) Blessed [fortunate, prosperous, and favored by God] is the man who does not walk in the counsel of the wicked [following their advice and example], nor stand in the path of sinners, nor sit [down to rest] in the seat of scoffers (ridiculers).
Proverbs 13:20 (NLT) Walk with the wise and become wise; associate with fools and get in trouble.
Proverbs 17:17 (AMP) A friend loves at all times and a brother is born for adversity.
Proverbs 18:24 (NIV) One who has unreliable friends soon comes to ruin, but there is a friend who sticks closer than a brother.
Proverbs 22:24 and 25 (NIV) Do not make friends with a hot-tempered person, do not associate with one easily angered, or you may learn their ways and get yourself ensnared.
Proverbs 27:6 (AMP) Faithful are the wounds of a friend [who corrects out of love and concern], but the kisses of an enemy are deceitful [because they serve his hidden agenda].
1 Corinthians 15:33 (NIV) Do not be misled: "Bad company corrupts good character."
Hebrews 10:24 (NLT) Let us think of ways to motivate one another to acts of love and good works.

If you desire marriage or are currently married and want your covenant to be in alignment with God's standard, then **Ephesians 5 (AMP)** is a good place to start. Paul instructs married couples to *submit to one another* and he explains what submission looks like for the wife and the husband, beginning at verse 22:

Wives, be *subject* to your own husbands, as [a service] to the Lord. For the husband is head of the wife, as Christ is head of the church, Himself *being* the Savior of the body. But as the church is subject to Christ, so also wives should be subject to their husbands in everything [respecting both their position as protector and their responsibility to God as head of the house].
Husbands, love your wives [seek the highest good for her and surround her with a caring, unselfish love], just as Christ also loved the church and gave Himself up for her, so that He might sanctify the church, having cleansed her by the washing of water with the word [of God], so that [in turn] He might present the church to Himself in glorious splendor, without spot or wrinkle or any such thing; but that she would be holy [set apart for God] and blameless. Even so husbands should *and* are morally obligated to love their own wives as [being in a sense] their own bodies. He who loves his own wife loves himself. For no one ever hated his own body, but [instead] he nourishes *and* protects and cherishes it, just as Christ does the church, because we are members (parts) of His body. FOR THIS REASON A MAN

SHALL LEAVE HIS FATHER AND HIS MOTHER AND SHALL BE JOINED [and be faithfully devoted] TO HIS WIFE, AND THE TWO SHALL BECOME ONE FLESH. This mystery [of two becoming one] is great; but I am speaking with reference to [the relationship of] Christ and the church. However, each man among you [without exception] is to love his wife as his very own self [with behavior worthy of respect and esteem, always seeking the best for her with an attitude of lovingkindness], and the wife [must see to it] that she respects *and* delights in her husband [that she notices him and prefers him and treats him with loving concern, treasuring him, honoring him, and holding him dear].

Be prepared to discuss the Scriptures listed on page 19. Feel free to use the space below for any comments or questions.

_____

_____

_____

_____

_____

_____

_____

_____

_____

Identity is an area of continual spiritual attack, not just in your relationships with others, but your relationship with God and yourself. Satan will attack your identity and he's coming to see if you know what God has spoken and if you believe it. In other words, *are you convinced that God's word is true, or can you be deceived into believing something else?* This is a tactic that the enemy has used since the beginning of time, while Adam and Eve were in the garden. He came to see if she knew God's word and then successfully deceived her, which led to the fall of mankind (see **Genesis 3**). Satan attempted the same tactic with Jesus generations later, this time in the wilderness. **Matthew 4:1-11 (AMP)** says,

> Then Jesus was led by the [Holy] Spirit into the wilderness to be tempted by the devil. After He had gone without food for forty days and forty nights, He became hungry. And the tempter came and said to Him, "If You are the Son of God, command that these stones become bread." But Jesus replied, "It is written *and* forever remains written, 'MAN SHALL NOT LIVE BY BREAD ALONE, BUT BY EVERY WORD THAT COMES OUT OF THE MOUTH OF GOD.' Then the devil took Him into the holy city [Jerusalem] and placed Him on the pinnacle (highest point) of the temple. And he said [mockingly] to Him, "If You are the Son of God, throw Yourself down; for it is written, 'HE WILL COMMAND HIS ANGELS CONCERNING YOU [to serve, care for, protect and watch over You]'and 'THEY WILL LIFT YOU UP ON *their* HANDS, SO THAT YOU WILL NOT STRIKE YOUR FOOT AGAINST A STONE.' Jesus said to him, "On the other hand, it is written *and* forever remains written, 'YOU SHALL NOT TEST THE LORD YOUR GOD.'" Again, the devil took Him up on a very high mountain and showed Him all the kingdoms of the world and the glory [splendor, magnificence, and excellence] of them; **and** he said to Him, "All these things I will give You, if You fall down and worship me." Then Jesus said to him, "Go away, Satan! For it is written *and* forever remains written, 'YOU SHALL WORSHIP THE LORD YOUR GOD, AND SERVE HIM ONLY.'" Then the devil left Him; and angels came and ministered to Him [bringing Him food and serving Him].

*Activity: What stands out to you in the above account? What do you see happening in this exchange between Jesus and Satan? What is Jesus' response to Satan? How would you respond if you were in Jesus' place? Answer in the space provided below

_____

_____

_____

_____

_____

_____

_____

_____

_____

_____

Notice that Satan comes to attack Jesus with the use of God's word, which means Satan knows the Word of God. Not only that, but he's crafty and *takes it out of context*. For example, the Scripture that he quotes to Jesus is actually from **Psalm 91,** which speaks about the blessing and protection reserved for those who trust God, and as it says in verse 9, *because you have made the LORD, [who is] my refuge, Even the Most High, your dwelling place…* However, Satan argues that this same protection will be present if Jesus yields to his command. Jesus knows that the Father's desire is for us to be obedient to His voice, not the voice of Satan.

Context is important when reading Scripture and Satan knows that. For example, the end of **Matthew 3** puts the events of Matthew 4 in context. Jesus is baptized by His cousin, John the Baptist. As Jesus comes out of the water Matthew shares, *…and behold, the heavens were opened, and he (John) saw the Spirit of God descending as a dove and lighting on Him (Jesus), and behold, a voice from heaven said, "This is My beloved Son, in whom I am well-pleased and delighted!"* **(AMP).** Jesus is not only baptized, but His identity is declared and affirmed by the Father. Given what we know about Satan, it should be no surprise to us as readers that he comes to attack the very words that were spoken over Jesus forty days prior by the Father. If he did it to Jesus, know that he is waiting for an opportune time to do the same to you. *What will your response be?* Will you take time to study the Word? Are you convinced of the truth of who God is and who you are in Him, or will the enemy succeed in deceiving you?

Notes from the author – *As previously stated, divorce is part of my story*. My marriage lasted four and a half years, two of which were spent in separation. As you can imagine, I was left with many questions and intense emotions. Some of those emotions were disappointment, exhaustion, unforgiveness, and, to my surprise, grief. I grieved every expectation that was never met and the reality that I was left with. I grieved the fact that I wasn't going to break the chain of divorce in my family. I saw how divorce impacted the hearts of my parents. Before them, my grandparents got a divorce, and maybe even the generation before that. I thought the cycle would end with me. I found myself asking God, *How do you feel about me?* The Word is clear, He hates the effects of divorce on the heart (see **Malachi 2** and **Matthew 19**). Yet still, I needed to be clear on how He felt about **me**. *Lord, do you forgive me,* and *are you willing to help me forgive myself? Do you still desire a relationship with me? Do you still have a plan for my life?*

While struggling under the weight of reality, the Lord showed me two things:

1st: *Jesus had to come home with me*. Getting the answers to those questions required more than Sunday service, small groups and serving. The investments I made in my horizontal relationships (friends and family) needed to be present in my vertical relationship (Jesus).

2nd: *I needed to heal*. That may sound trite, but healing transformed my relationship with God. I'll expound on healing in the next section.

Part IV: Who Does God Say You Are?

In Part I, we discussed some of the qualities of God. We are made, as stated in Genesis 1, in His image – so our lives should mirror the qualities that reflect His divine nature. Yet, the Lord also tells us who we are directly. He formed us and breathed life into us, and His Word guides us into seeing and valuing ourselves accurately. I've heard it said, *if you don't understand the reason for the existence of a thing, then misuse is inevitable*. Understanding comes when you take time to read the manual. For example, if you try to pair a remote to a TV it's not made for, the result will be limited functionality. Limited because there are some features that remain inaccessible to the user due to the incorrect pairing. The manual was not considered. However, even if a remote is paired with the correct TV – how many individuals access the complete range of amenities that it offers? I would argue slim to none, because most times programming ceases once basic needs are met. The manual is either not read at all or considered only after an avoidable issue arises. This is why reading the manual is so imperative, whether it's a remote or something else to ensure proper use and safeguard against misuse.

Apply this principle to your relationships. If you don't read the manual God's given in the form of the Bible to discover who He says you are, then ignorance of how you should treat yourself and others is inevitable. That ignorance or lack of awareness often leads to abuse. How many people have gone through life being abused: emotionally, mentally, spiritually or physically? How many have abused others simply because they didn't read the manual? Or they read the manual but never apply the instructions to their life. Prayerfully, the following Scriptures will challenge your beliefs about yourself and others. Beyond that, my prayer is that God's Word will inform you of who He is and what He sees when He looks at you.

You are a Masterpiece: **Ephesians 2:10 (NLT)**

You are His Bride and You are Redeemed: **Isaiah 54:5 (NIV) and Ephesians 1:7 (NIV)**

You are Royalty: **1 Peter 2:9-10 (NIV)**

You are Fearfully and Wonderfully Made: **Psalm 139: 13-14 (NIV)**

You are Chosen: **John 15:16 (NIV) and Ephesians 1:11-12 (NIV)**

You are Marked and Sealed by His Spirit: **Ephesians 1:13-14 (NIV)**

You are an Ambassador of Christ: **2 Corinthians 5:19-20 (AMP)**

You are a Child of God: **1 John 3:1 (NIV)**

You are Loved and Forgiven: **Ephesians 4:32, 5:1-2 (NIV) and 1 John 4:9-10 (NIV)**

This is not an exhaustive list, but it serves as an introduction to *who you are*. Meditate on these passages until your heart learns to believe and comes into agreement with the truth.

Be prepared to discuss the Scriptures. Feel free to use the space below for your comments and/or questions.

_____

_____

_____

_____

_____

_____

_____

_____

_____

Notes from the author –*Part III ended with the Lord showing me that I needed to heal.* You may wonder, *how did she know it was God?* First, God desires for us to be healed from the snares and destruction of sin and walk in freedom and wholeness (see **Isaiah 53 AMP**). So when I sensed a strong urge to heal in my spirit, I knew it was God drawing me because healing aligns with His Word and nature. The second reason is personal – healing was not something that I had context for, nor did I know what it looked like in practice. Before marriage, "healing" consisted of distractions. If I wasn't in a relationship, then I had a crush. If I didn't have a crush, then someone had a crush on me and since I valued attention, I entertained it. My heart was a relational dumping ground from middle school until marriage. The funny thing is, I never really felt satisfied or content, but it was easy and familiar. When the divorce was final and I stepped into singleness again, the Lord made one thing clear: He wanted to break a dysfunctional cycle in my life. I chose to yield to His will, and the process was humbling, agitating, and required a profound acquaintance with the weight and depth of my emotions.

Discovering the extent of healing meant that I had to first assess what was broken, because the cycle was only a symptom. I became aware of my dad's relational patterns. When I reflect on my formative years, there was almost always someone else in the picture. Whether it was a girlfriend who lived with him or women he casually dated or brought around, this became a consistent thread. He modeled behaviors that I'd eventually invite into my own life. The Lord didn't just open my eyes to generational implications, but to what I believed about Him and myself. I felt valued when a man wanted: my body, mind, time, company, and affection. In those moments, I felt seen, loved, and worthy, even though the undercurrent of dissatisfaction remained. What needed to be healed was my grieved heart and mind once I realized what was guiding my decisions: the dopamine high that I got from attention…every flirtatious comment, wink, smile, kiss, and embrace made me feel more seen and less lonely. I worshipped Jesus and sang songs about Him being more than enough, but in reality, I wasn't living like He was. *I had to repent.* Repent for not trusting Him with my heart and for not believing that He's enough. Repent for not valuing my own heart or the hearts of others.

I was living the Scripture a hope deferred makes the heart sick (**Proverbs 13:12 NIV**). Marriage let me down in ways that I simply was not prepared for, largely because I went into it selfishly and ignorantly. However, the sobering realization of failed expectations and the mental and emotional toll that divorce takes felt overwhelming. There was even a young man that the Lord allowed me to reconnect with around that time, but it wasn't for the purpose of dating. Still, my heart didn't know the difference. I felt drawn to him and desired to lean back into that familiar cycle. Jesus kept every door shut when it came to that becoming anything more than a friendship. That young man would go on to play a pivotal role in leading me closer to God.

So, other than repentance, what did healing look like practically? I intentionally sought out things that fed and nurtured my spirit because I was fighting discouragement. I listened to praise and worship music in my car, my office, and at the gym. I listened to sermons by trusted pastors, some of whom were referred by the aforementioned young man. Those teachings challenged my mindset and the story I told myself about my worth, value, and future. Some of those sermons brought clarity and language to the waves of emotions I felt throughout marriage, but they also helped move me along the path of unlearning. There were things that I envisioned and believed for myself that were not grounded in God's Word. For example, I never believed that I would be a homeowner without a husband. In my mind, homeownership and marriage went hand-in-hand, and I wasn't willing to concede. For the first time, I had to embrace the reality that that may not be my story. Coming to grips with my underlying beliefs forced me to continue to examine my relationship with God: *do I need a husband to accomplish this, or is Jesus enough?*

Adding things to my life that encouraged my spirit and trust in God was not sufficient on its own. I also needed to starve the things that fed the desires of my flesh. I stopped listening to R&B songs that fed the unhealthy desire for attention in me. I began phasing out secular rap music and I took a break from romantic comedies and romance movies in general. I also had to distance myself a bit from the young man that my heart was so drawn to, until I could emotionally find my footing again. This may sound extreme to some, but God made the focus clear: this portion of my healing journey was to consist of Him and me, no distractions. It was my responsibility to disconnect from the things that pulled me away from that focus.

Simultaneously, I was consistently reading God's word. Jesus tells us clearly in His conversation with Pharisees (religious leaders) in **Matthew 12:34 (NLT)**...*For whatever is in your heart determines what you say. A good person produces good things from the treasury of a good heart, and an evil person produces evil things from the treasury of an evil heart.* In order for the story I believed about my life to evolve, the source of the information needed to change. I fed my spirit, mind, and heart the life-giving truth of God's Word. For the first time, I began listening to the Word – yes, *you read that right! I wasn't just reading my Bible, I listened to it on Bible Gateway* – and spent a lot of time in the Old Testament, to get a deeper understanding of God's nature.

I looked for Scriptures that spoke directly to who God is and who He says I am. There were four that spoke to me. I wrote them down, hung them up over my bed, and meditated on them every morning, night, and periodically throughout the day. This was my rhythm for several months. Looking back, I realize that's what it took for my heart to release the lies that were spoken over me by my ex-husband, family members, and myself, and to embrace the truth of who God says I am. This is how I learned to hide the Word in my heart (**Psalm 119:11**). When it comes to embracing your God-given identity *there is no way* to do it without consistent meditation on God's Word. Whether you are a veteran of the faith or you have yet to receive Jesus as your Lord and Savior, this is something that we are all called to do. This is the process of coming out of agreement with the world's definitions of identity and choosing to align yourself with truth. Ask the Holy Spirit to help you cultivate a love for the Word, patience, and consistency as you grow in your trust and faith in Jesus.

The more time I spent with Him, the more I learned to trust His nature and heart. The more I trusted, the more I valued His presence and began to believe that He is more than enough. Jesus is a safe space for the darkest and most fragile places of my heart. I pray that you will experience this level of intimacy and safety with the one who created you, breathed life into your lungs and loves you more deeply than words can describe.

For those who are curious, the Scriptures that I wrote down and are still hanging over my bed are:

Psalm 100:3 (NIV) - Know that the LORD is God. It is He who made us, and we are His, we are His people, the sheep of His pasture.

Psalm 139:14 (NIV) - I praise you because I am fearfully and wonderfully made; your works are wonderful, I know that full well.

Isaiah 43:1(NKJV) - Fear not, for I have redeemed you; I have called *you* by your name; You *are* Mine.

1 John 3:1 (NIV) - See what great love the Father has lavished on us, that we should be called children of God! And that is what we are!

Search the scriptures for yourself on God's nature and who He says you are and write down the verses that grab you. Start your journey of meditating on His Word and come out of agreement with the lies that have been spoken over you. Choose to align yourself with the truth of the one who created you.

*__Activity__: As a group or individually, purchase some 3x5 index cards and write the Scriptures down that resonate with you. Keep them with you and meditate on them daily. Ask the Holy Spirit for help in making those Scriptures a reality in your heart, mind and life.

If you walk this process out for yourself, then expect to discover who you are as you seek the face and heart of God. He'll remind you of where you came from. He'll minister to the fragile areas of your heart and mind, and He'll reveal how He's been preparing you for this moment and what is to come. In His timing, you will discover who you are, why you're here, and where you are going. I echo the prophetic words of Paul, *and I am certain that God, who began the good work within you, will continue His work until it is finally finished on the day when Christ Jesus returns* (**Philippians 1:6 NLT**).

Part V: Now What?

There has been a lot of information shared throughout the previous sections and I pray that this curriculum has planted the seed of identity in your heart. Not only that, but I pray that it has led to vulnerable conversations and deep soul work. The intention behind this is for communities to get together to discover or be reminded of the truth of who they are. If you read this as part of a small group, a Bible study curriculum, a book club or with your significant other or friends – great! But, don't let the journey stop here. The next step can be creating a vision board. For those who have never made a vision board, it is a collage of images and words that serve as inspiration or motivation of some goal or belief that you have. People tend to create vision boards for financial goals, entrepreneurial goals or milestones they want to achieve annually. While this is culture's template, what does God say about vision?

Then the LORD answered me and said, "Write the vision and engrave it plainly on [clay] tablets so that the one who reads it will run. For the vision is yet for the appointed [future] time. It hurries toward the goal [of fulfillment]; it will not fail. Even though it delays, wait [patiently] for it, because it will certainly come; it will not delay" **(Habakkuk 2:2-3 AMP)**.

In this account of Scripture, the Old Testament prophet relays a word from God as it relates to vision. Write it down with enough clarity that someone else can read it and run, or have enough understanding of the vision to act on it. After engaging with this curriculum, I pray that you're starting to see yourself free of culture's expectations on who you're supposed to be. Prayerfully, you've started challenging the lies that family members, ex-spouses or significant others, friend groups or bosses have spoken over your life.

Now it's time to write down who God says you are. Picture yourself whole, free and full of peace and gratitude. What is it going to take to make that vision a reality? As mentioned in the previous section, the Word is your launching pad, but beyond that, what do you need to walk out your identity on the earth? If nothing comes to mind, pray and ask God to show you. Write down what He reveals on a vision board and keep it in a visible place. This will keep your focus clear, and help you extend grace and patience to yourself as you walk out your own transformation in Christ. The vision board will also serve as ammunition in your fight against the craftiness of Satan as he tries to destroy your trust in God and your assurance of who you are in Him.

For those who've read this curriculum in a class setting, retreat, or alone – I encourage you to seek out godly community that's walking in their true identity or desires to learn about their identity in Christ. As you will read in the Acknowledgments, this kind of work cannot be done alone. You need people who will speak to the king or queen on the inside of you. People who see your blind spots and won't allow you to disqualify yourself. People who will challenge you, encourage you, and remind you of what God says when your heart is tempted to stray. *See to it, brothers and sisters, that none of you has a sinful, unbelieving heart that turns away from the living God. But encourage one another daily, as long as it is called Today, so that none of you may be hardened by sin's deceitfulness* **(Hebrews 3:12-13 NIV)**. Our hearts are so sensitive and we as people are complex, fickle and temperamental. As long as we are living in this fallen world, not only do we have Satan to contend with, but we have our own sinful nature that's crouching at the door of our heart **(Genesis 4:7)**. Nevertheless, we have hope and help through Jesus Christ. When we confess our sins and receive His Holy Spirit, He gives us the power and the will to obey **(Philippians 2:13)**. God does transformative and sanctifying work in us as individuals, but we get a full picture of His grace, love and kindness when we choose to be part of a community. If you try to do this faith walk alone it's only a matter of time before you lose heart, get tired and lean back into what's familiar and easy. In most cases the easy way leads to dysfunction and dissatisfaction. Allow God to guide you through the process of breaking old cycles and mindsets. Pursue intimacy with Christ and faith-filled communities that will hold you accountable and help you walk out the assignments and calling on your life.

Acknowledgments

Certain things happen in life that you look at and say, *Wow! I didn't see that coming*. Writing this curriculum has been one of those things. Who would have thought that the Lord would birth this through me? While I am in awe and amazement of what He has done and continues to do, I realize that it took a village.

Thank you, *Ms. Carolyn Haygood*. I've heard Pastor Daniels say *some of God's greatest blessings will walk into your life on two legs*. If that quote was a person, it would be you. You have been a blessing to me since meeting you in 2020, when you became my small group coach. Every conversation we've had since has been full of wisdom, laughter, truth, love and transparency. Not only have we endured some of life's greatest heartaches, but we have equally experienced the strength, grace, healing and sanctifying power of God through it all. I'm grateful that God brought us together in this stage of life. Although we are in different seasons, we are both committed to living lives that are worthy of the calling that God has given us. We share a commitment of going deeper: not just in our knowledge of Christ, but in our love and affection towards Him as well. Knowing that we both share the same burden for helping people discover and walk out their identity in Christ through intimacy with Him has helped me to keep saying yes to God throughout this journey. This ministry is so much bigger than us, but in God's kindness, He sends like-minded people to help us remain steadfast and to remind us that we are not alone. Every prayer, every conversation, every Scripture written or declared, and every sermon watched were divinely orchestrated and has brought us to this place. I look forward to the partnership and the continued depth that God will produce through our relationship. God has allowed us to run this race of faith together and *for that I am full of praise and gratitude*. What a mighty and mindful God we serve.

Thank you to my coach, *Mrs. Shan Mitchum*. I came to you in October 2023 with a burden in my heart. At that time, I told you I needed either therapy or a coach. I wasn't completely sure which one, but I knew I needed help in making that burden something tangible. You stepped in, made space for me, listened intently and offered your wisdom and expertise to help me create a workshop that bears the same title as this body of work. You challenged me, asked thought provoking questions and spoke life into me throughout every step of this process. Without your obedience to God in saying yes to guiding me, this would still be just an idea.

Thank you to *Mrs. Khas Cody*. God placed us in each other's life at the exact time that I began to realize that He is calling me to teach and that He's assigning me to young women who are void of an understanding and conviction of their identity. The conversations we had in the office of The Father's House Church about relationships, worth, value and identity all helped in stirring the fire that the Holy Spirit was kindling within me. If there was ever a moment when fear wanted to paralyze me or I doubted going in this direction, our conversations reminded me to keep leaning in. *For that I am grateful.*

Lastly, thank you to my faith-filled communities. My small group co-lead, *Ms. Sarah Herbert*, thank you for your consistent prayers and holding me accountable. Thank you to my small group members who made space for me to not only talk about this ministry, but also participated in evaluations, discussions around identity and the workshop. Leading this small group has filled me in ways that I couldn't have fathomed. I am so grateful that God assigned me to it and for every woman that has been part of and is currently part of this community. Thank you *Mrs. Carey Tanzola* and the ladies in her small group who prayed over this ministry and supported it.

Thank you to *Mr. Willie Jones III* for challenging me, praying with and for me, and encouraging me. When God started pulling me in the direction of teaching, I wasn't ready to accept it. Whenever someone mentioned my name and teaching in the same sentence, my response was *I'm not a teacher.* My willingness to say yes was buried somewhere between fear and denial. You told me sternly yet in love, *stop saying what you're not.* Your tone and the directness of that statement was exactly what I needed to hear, and those words are repeated in the track of my mind to this day. You have watched this curriculum grow from a seed to a ministry that others can glean from, and you've helped keep me accountable throughout the process. Thank you for listening. Thank you for prophesying. Thank you for being a faithful friend.

Thank you *Mrs. Amanda Williams, Mrs. Beverly Barcliffe, Ms. Laquanda Fields and Mrs. Shameka Zarcone.* Every time we get together the Holy Spirit moves and stirs our hearts. While we are in different places in our journey, we are all stepping out of the boat together and encouraging and praying for each other with every step. *I prayed for communities like this* and God has been faithful to answer.

As we all continue to work out our salvation and lean into whatever God has assigned us to, I pray that we continue to stir each other on in our faith and keep this in the forefront of our hearts and minds…*for it is God who works in you to will and to act in order to fulfill His good purpose.* As this curriculum grows so will the village and I'm excited for the journey. This is just the beginning. *There is still so much work to do.*

Identity is far too deep and rich to capture in just *thirty-six* pages. It forms the foundation of our lives, and learning to embrace it—and walk confidently in it through life's many seasons—can often feel overwhelming.

You have journeyed with me through revelation, unlearning, and the discovery of my own identity in Christ, but it cannot stop here. What you've read so far is only the groundwork. *Now it's time to hear other voices.* The voices of those navigating different seasons: individuals who have endured heartache and chose to bring their pain to the feet of Jesus; those who have been healed or are actively walking out their healing and, in the process, discovering who God has called them to be; and those who have experienced the crown of beauty instead of ashes, the oil of joy instead of mourning, and have put on the garment of praise instead of settling in heaviness and despair **(Isaiah 61 NIV)**.

As grateful and elated as I am that God led me through this process —and that these words are now in your hands to glean from—He has made it clear that this is only the beginning. Whether discovering or *rediscovering* identity through marriage, parenthood, grief, or success, this work began *with a village,* and God will *use a village* to bring it to completion.

Be on the lookout for the next installment.

About the Author

Jordyn Larkins is a follower of Jesus who is passionate about helping people discover and embrace their true identity. Having personally endured the pain of misplaced identity and the freedom that comes with clarity, she writes to guide others toward a deeper understanding of who and *Whose* they are.

A native of Upstate New York, she is active in her local church, is known for her infectious laugh, and desires to use her gifts to reflect God's truth, deepen faith, and guide readers to transformed lives.

Jordyn studied Communications and Media at Alfred University and Syracuse University. She has experience in radio broadcasting and audio editing, but has since transitioned to municipal budget development. After stepping away from writing for several years, the Lord called her back to it, rekindling a gift that is now a vital piece of her ministry.

Notes

Introduction

1. Hosea 4:6 (AMP)

Part I: Who I am, Why I'm Here & Where I'm Going…

1. Genesis 1:27 (AMP)
2. 1 John 4: 7-12(NIV)
3. 1 Peter 1:15 (NIV)
4. Psalm 8:4 (NIV)
5. 1 Thessalonians 5:24 (NIV)
6. Hebrews 13:8 (NIV)
7. Colossians 3:13 (NIV)
8. Psalm 103:13 (AMP)
9. 2 Peter 3:9 (NIV)
10. Romans 11:22 (NIV)
11. Exodus 33:14 (NIV)
12. "Identity." *Merriam-Webster.com Dictionary*, Merriam-Webster, https://www.merriam-webster.com/dictionary/identity. Accessed 13 Nov. 2025.

Part II: Cultivating a Relationship with God

1. Joshua 1:9 (NLT)
2. Psalm 32:5 (NIV)
3. 1 Samuel 8:19-20 (NIV)
4. 1 Samuel 12:20-22 (NIV)
5. Acts 2:37-38 (NIV)
6. James 4:8 (NIV)
7. RedefinedTV. (n.d.). Home [@BeRedefined]. YouTube. Retrieved November 13, 2025 from https://www.youtube.com/@Beredefined

Part III: Identity and Impact

1. Daniels, Dharius. *Your Purpose is Calling: Your Difference is Your Destiny*. Grand Rapids, MI: Zondervan, 20 Sept. 2022.
2. Matthew 28:19-20 (NIV)
3. Mark 16: 15-16 (NIV)

4. Ephesians 4:1 (NLT)
5. 2 Thessalonians 1:11-12 (AMP)
6. 2 Timothy 1:9 (AMP)
7. 1 Peter 3:8-9 (AMP)
8. Luke 9:1 (AMP)
9. John 15:16 (AMP)
10. Ephesians 4:1 (NIV)
11. 1 Peter 3:8 (AMP)
12. Romans 11:29 (AMP)
13. Jeremiah 29:11 (NIV)
14. Psalm 1:1 (AMP)
15. Proverbs 13:20 (NLT)
16. Proverbs 17:17 (AMP)
17. Proverbs 18:24 (NIV)
18. Proverbs 22:24-25 (NIV)
19. Proverbs 27:6 (AMP)
20. 1 Corinthians 15:33 (NIV)
21. Hebrews 10:24 (NLT)
22. Ephesians 5:22-33 (AMP)
23. Genesis 3:6-24 (NIV)
24. Matthew 4:1-11 (AMP)
25. Psalm 91:9-12 (AMP)
26. Matthew 3:13-17 (AMP)
27. Malachi 2:16 (NIV)
28. Matthew 19:8 (NIV)

Part IV: Who Does God Say You Are?

1. Genesis 1:26 (NIV)
2. Ephesians 2:10 (NLT)
3. Isaiah 54:4 (NIV)
4. Ephesians 1:7 (NIV)
5. 1 Peter 2:9-10 (NIV)
6. Psalm 139:13-14 (NIV)
7. John 15:16 (NIV)
8. Ephesians 1:11-12 (NIV)
9. Ephesians 1:13-14 (NIV)
10. 2 Corinthians 5:19-20 (AMP)

11. 1 John 3:1 (NIV)
12. Ephesians 4:32 (NIV)
13. Ephesians 5:1-2 (NIV)
14. 1 John 4:9-10 (NIV)
15. Isaiah 53:5 (AMP)
16. Proverbs 13:12 (NIV)
17. Matthew 12:34 (NLT)
18. Psalm 119:11 (NIV)
19. Psalm 100:3 (NIV)
20. Psalm 139:14 (NIV)
21. Isaiah 43:1 (NIV)
22. 1 John 3:1 (NIV)
23. Philippians 1:6 (NLT)

Part V: Now What?

1. Habakkuk 2:2-3 (AMP)
2. Hebrews 3:12-13 (NIV)
3. Genesis 4:7 (NIV)
4. Philippians 2:13 (NIV)

Acknowledgments

1. Philippians 2:13 (NIV)

Discovering Identity Through…

1. Isaiah 61:3 (NIV)